Leaders and Allies Matter

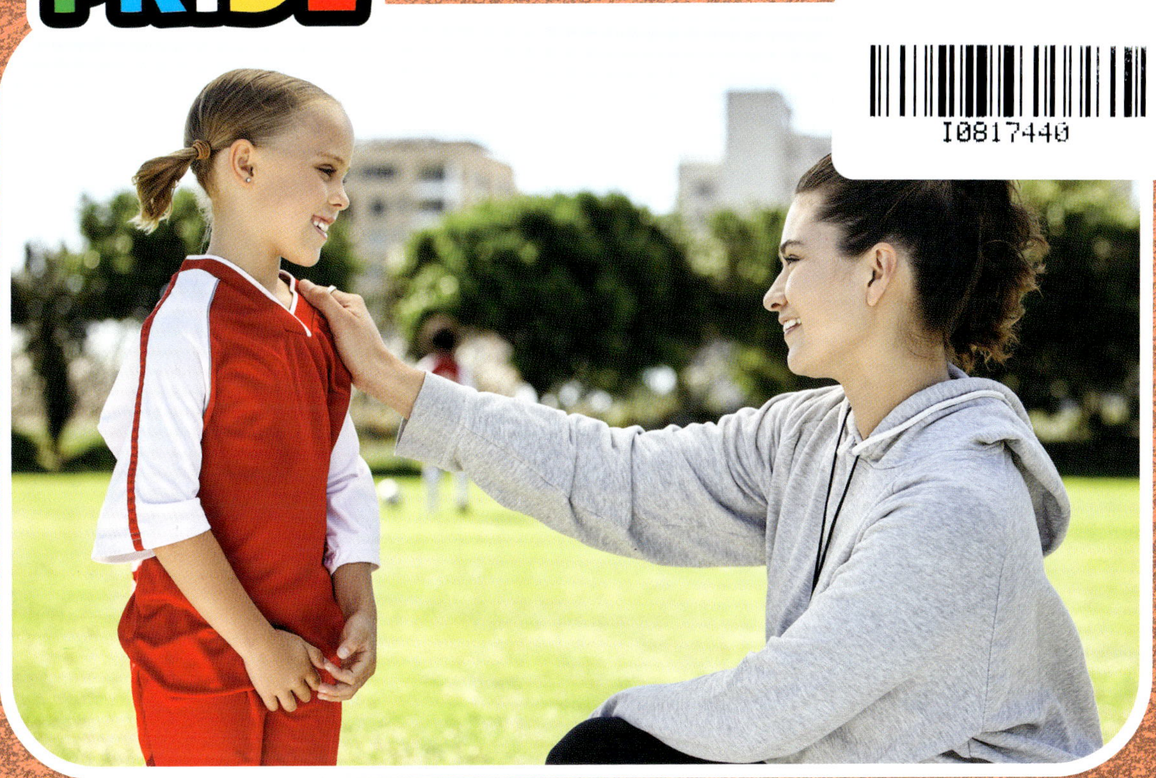

Juliana Burkhart

PowerKiDS press

Published in 2025 by The Rosen Publishing Group, Inc.
2544 Clinton Street, Buffalo, NY 14224

Editor: Michele Suchomel-Casey
Book Design: Leslie Taylor

Photo Credits: Cover PeopleImages.com - Yuri A/Shutterstock.com; (series background) P.siripak/Shutterstock.com; (series disability pride colors) rudall30/Shutterstock.com; p. 5 1st footage/Shutterstock.com, p. 5 (inset flag) Maxim Studio/Shutterstock.com; p. 6 Jaren Jai Wicklund/Shutterstock.com; p. 7 Ermolaev Alexander/Shutterstock.com; p. 9 Raph_PH/File:LizzoBrixt06Nov19-10 (49216792848) (cropped).jpg/commons.wikimedia.org; p. 11 Cvandyke/Shutterstock.com, (inset) East Asia and Pacific Media Hub U.S. Department of State/File:Judith Heumann, from- Ambassadors Kennedy Greets Sp. Advisor for Disability Rights Heumann in Tokyo - Flickr - East Asia and Pacific Media Hub (1) (cropped).jpg/commons.wikimedia.org; p. 13 Sipa USA/Alamy.com; p. 14 Rick Guidotti for Positive Exposure/Photo provided by Sora Kasuga; p. 15 Rose Marincil/Photo provided by Sora Kasuga; p. 16 SNCC Political Education Materials by Courtland Cox and Jennifer Lawson/File:Lowndes County Freedom Organization flyer (cropped).jpg/commons.wikimedia.org; p. 17 YAKOBCHUK VIACHESLAV/Shutterstock.com; p. 19 JOKE_PHATRAPONG/Shutterstock.com; p. 21 wavebreakmedia/Shutterstock.com.

Cataloging-in-Publication Data

Names: Burkhart, Juliana.
Title: Leaders and allies matter / Juliana Burkhart.
Description: Buffalo, NY : PowerKids Press, 2025. | Series: Disability pride | Includes glossary and index.
Identifiers: ISBN 9781499446869 (pbk.) | ISBN 9781499446876 (library bound) | ISBN 9781499446883 (ebook)
Subjects: LCSH: People with disabilities--Political activity--Juvenile literature. | People with disabilities--Civil rights--Juvenile literature. | Discrimination against people with disabilities--Juvenile literature.
Classification: LCC HV1568.B87 2025 | DDC 362.4--dc23

Manufactured in the United States of America

Some of the images in this book illustrate individuals who are models. The depictions do not imply actual situations or events.

CPSIA Compliance Information: Batch #CSPK25. For Further Information contact Rosen Publishing at 1-800-237-9932.

Contents

Celebrating Diversity

What would the world be like if everyone looked the same, talked the same, and had the same ideas? It would probably be pretty boring! **Diversity** is when people of different races, genders, abilities, or cultures feel included. We celebrate diversity because our different experiences make us special and strong.

Some people are afraid of others who are different from them. They don't like to see people who wear different clothes, have different bodies, or speak different languages. Sometimes people are treated unfairly because they are different. This is called **discrimination**. Discrimination is very hurtful, because it can prevent someone from living a safe and happy life.

The disability pride flag was created to show acceptance and respect for people who have disabilities. Each color is for a different type of disability.

- The gray background is in honor of those who've died.
- Green is for disabilities that have to do with the senses.
- Blue is for those that have to with the mind and emotions.
- White stands for unseen disabilities, as well as those that haven't been diagnosed, or found out.
- Gold is for neurodiversity.
- Red is for other disabilities of the body.

A disability is a condition that limits or changes what a person can do or the way they can do it. Some disabilities affect the senses or movement. Other disabilities affect how people think and learn. Sometimes disabilities are visible; sometimes they're not.

What Is an Ally?

We all need friends who support us when we need help. An ally is a special kind of friend who promises to stand up for fairness. An ally notices when someone is being treated badly because they are different. An ally wants to learn about what they can do to help make sure everyone is treated equally.

An ally gives everyone an equal chance to speak their mind and share their point of view.

Anyone can use their voice to speak up for fairness, but some people get to use their voice more than others. This is called **privilege**. An ally uses their privilege to help those with less privilege make their voices heard.

Abled privilege is the privilege non-disabled people have. For example, a person with a disability may need help with everyday tasks, such as dressing and brushing their teeth. A non-disabled person can do these tasks without help.

Learning to Be an Ally

Being an ally is something you have to practice your whole life. When you're learning to be an ally, you might make mistakes and hurt someone else's feelings. They might even get angry with you. You might feel angry or hurt too. But mistakes are opportunities to learn.

Some mistakes happen when your intent is different than your impact. Your intent is what you mean to do when you act. Your impact is the result of your actions. The impact of our actions on others is more important than our intent. **Apologize** if you hurt someone, and try to learn how to be a better ally.

In 2022, pop star Lizzo released an edited version of her song "Grrls." This was in response from fans who complained the she had used an offensive term for people with disabilities. Lizzo apologized, and her fans appreciated it.

Learn More

The American Association of People with Disabilities (AAPD) is a group that supports the civil rights of Americans with disabilities. You can learn more about what they do at www.aapd.com.

Being a Leader

When she was a baby, Judy Heumann had a sickness called polio. After her illness, Judy used a wheelchair to get around. Her school wouldn't allow her wheelchair in the classroom, so her parents had to fight for her to get an education. Judy made friends at a summer camp for kids with disabilities. Her friends were also frustrated by the discrimination they faced in the world.

Judy grew up and became a leader by speaking publicly about the rights of individuals with disabilities. She wanted the United States to make disability rights a federal law.

Judy Heumann worked hard to make new laws for disability rights.

In 1977, Judy and around 150 protestors with disabilities and their allies refused to leave the U.S. Department of Health building in San Francisco for about 26 days. They wanted to see more legal protections for kids and adults with disabilities.

Judy went on to help develop civil rights laws while working for the mayor of Washington, D.C., and the president of the United States. You can be a leader like Judy by speaking up if you notice that someone with a disability doesn't have equal access at school or in public places.

We all have a unique perspective, or point of view, formed by our different life experiences. This shapes how we see the world and what we think of other people.

Judy Heumann (far left) and other disability rights activists attended the Academy Awards in 2021 to celebrate a documentary made about the summer camp where they met.

Practicing Empathy

Have you ever noticed that the bad guys in movies or video games often have scars on their faces? In real life, people with burns, scars, or other kinds of facial differences are not evil or weird, but they experience discrimination because of the way they look.

Sora J. Kasuga is a model and performer who was born with a facial difference that affects the left side of her face.

We are all different, but we all experience emotions like sadness, joy, embarrassment, and fear. When we try to understand someone else's feelings, we are practicing **empathy**. A good ally is empathetic and asks what they can do to help.

Sora's art and **advocacy** aims to portray people with facial differences as strong and beautiful. You can be an ally by helping your friends see physical differences as a normal part of being a person.

Sora J. Kasuga (shown here) aims to change the way people see performers with disabilities.

How Can You Be an Ally?

You can use your empathy to understand how someone else is feeling. But you can also use your eyes and ears to observe when someone is being **excluded**. You might see that someone always sits alone at lunch, or hear one of your peers use hurtful language when talking about a student with a disability.

The Black Panther Party was started in 1966 by two students, Bobby Seale and Huey P. Newton. The Black Panthers fought for equal rights for Black people. They also supported Judy Heumann's 1977 protest in San Francisco by bringing food and water to protestors with disabilities. The Black Panthers were allies in the fight for disability rights.

When you observe that someone else is hurting or alone, the first way you can be an ally is to be a friend. You can offer to sit with them or talk about their day. Simple kindness can go a long way toward making someone feel included.

An ally looks for signs that someone needs a friend. What do you see in this photo that tells you someone is being excluded?

Stay Safe

When you see someone else using words that hurt another person, the best thing to do is ignore the bully and practice kindness to the victim. You can invite them to go with you to another space away from the bully, or change the conversation to something else.

Sometimes discrimination takes the form of **violence**. If you see someone physically hurting another person, don't put yourself in danger to help. Call an adult you trust and ask them to help handle the situation safely.

Discrimination can take the form of physical violence, **threats**, or cyberbullying. If you see this, it's important to remember the facts so you can tell an adult what happened.

Never put yourself in an unsafe situation. You can only help if you stay safe.

First Steps

Are you ready to become a good ally in the disability community? An ally isn't something you can just say you are. Learning to be an ally takes practice. The first step is to listen to stories from people who are different from you. Use your empathy to understand how they feel. Can you think back to a time when you felt the same way?

Becoming a good ally is easier when you have others to learn with. Can you think of a friend or family member who might want to become a better ally? Talk to them about how you can practice together.

Showing kindness and empathy is the first step to becoming a good ally.

Glossary

advocacy: The act of supporting a cause.

apologize: To say you're sorry.

discrimination: When a person is treated unfairly because of their age, gender, race, culture, or ability.

diversity: The quality or state of having many different types, forms, or ideas.

empathy: The ability to understand and feel how someone else is feeling.

exclude: To keep out of something.

privilege: An advantage granted only to a particular person or group.

threat: An expression of the intent to harm someone or do something unwanted.

violence: The use of force in a way that harms a person or property.

For More Information

BOOKS

Feder, Tyler. *Bodies Are Cool*. New York, NY: Penguin Random House, 2021.

Gitlitz-Rapoport, Rebecca, and Sam Rapoport. *A Kid's Book About Allyship*. Portland, OR: A Kid's Book About, Inc., 2022.

Johnson, Chelsea, LaToya Council, and Carolyn Choi. *Intersection Allies: We Make Room for All*. New York, NY: Dottir Press, 2019.

WEBSITES

Kids Explain Allyship
www.youtube.com/watch?v=sZBUmq4EEf0
In their own words, these kids tell us what it means to be a good ally.

Teach Kids to Be Allies–Learn the 5 D's for Kids
parents-together.org/teach-kids-to-be-allies-learn-the-5-ds-for-kids/
Learn "the 5 D's" as tools for safe intervention in harassment situations.

Publisher's note to educators and parents: Our editors have carefully reviewed these websites to ensure that they are suitable for students. Many websites change frequently, however, and we cannot guarantee that a site's future contents will continue to meet our high standards of quality and educational value. Be advised that students should be closely supervised whenever they access the internet.

Index